Are You Ready for Bed?

pajamas

blanket

pillow

teddy bear

hug

kiss

lullaby

bedtime story

Are you ready for bed?

No, I need my pajamas.

Are you ready for bed?

No, I need my blanket.

Are you ready for bed?

No, I need my teddy bear.

Are you ready for bed?

No, I need a bedtime story.

Are you ready for bed?

No, I need a hug.

Are you ready for bed?

Yes. Good night!

Let's learn about Germany.

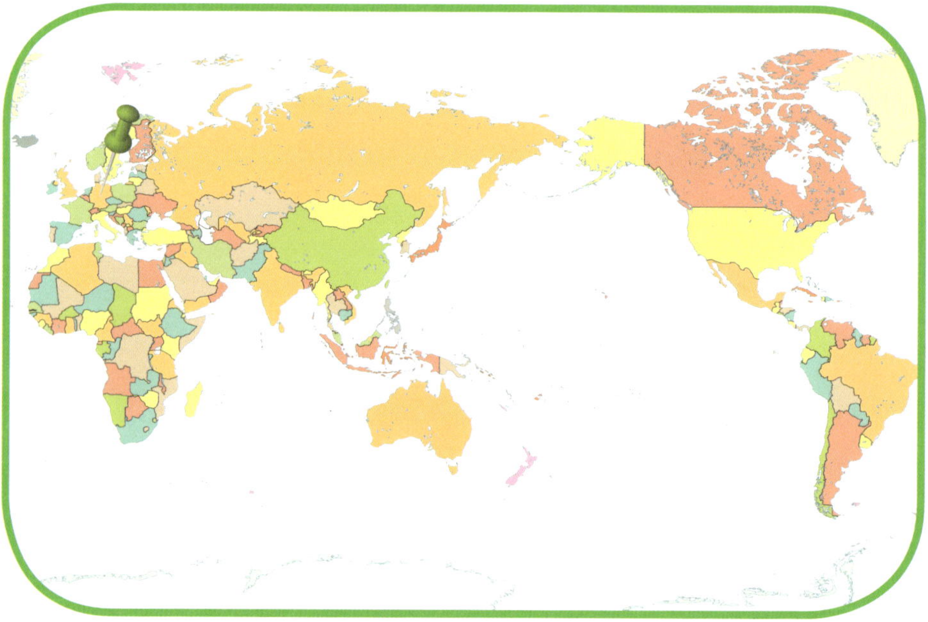

Flag of Germany

Grimm Brothers